Presented to

_____

By

_____

On the Occasion of

_____

Date

_____

© 2009 by Barbour Publishing, Inc.

Compiled by Kathy Shutt.

ISBN 978-1-60260-614-2

Several text selections were compiled from the following: *Moments of Adventure*, *Moments of Laughter*, *Moments of Understanding*, *Moments of Indulgence*, *Inspiration for Friends*, *Secrets of Beauty*, and *365 Favorite Quotes for Friends*, published by Barbour Publishing, Inc.

Published by Barbour Publishing, Inc., P.O. Box 719, Uhrichsville, Ohio 44683, www.barbourbooks.com

Our mission is to publish and distribute inspirational products offering exceptional value and biblical encouragement to the masses.

Member of the
Evangelical Christian
Publishers Association

Printed in India.

WHISPERS OF
Friendship

BARBOUR
PUBLISHING

A True Friend

A true friend unbosoms freely,
advises justly, assists readily,
adventures boldly, takes all
patiently, defends courageously,
and continues a friend
unchangeably.

WILLIAM PENN

Sunshine of Prosperity

The friends in my adversity I
shall always cherish most. I can
better trust those who helped to
relieve the gloom of my dark hours
than those who are so ready to
enjoy with me the sunshine of my
prosperity.

ULYSSES S. GRANT

Be Thankful for Friends

Dear God, thank You for my
friends. Help me not to take them
for granted. . . . Remind me often
how poor my life would be without
the friends You've given me. Help
me to enrich their lives as they
have mine. Amen.

One of God's Best Gifts

Blessed are they who have the gift
of making friends, for it is one of
God's best gifts. It involves many
things, but above all the power
of going out of one's self and
appreciating what is noble and
loving in another.

THOMAS HUGHES

Kindness and Compassion

It is not part of God's plan that
each one of us has beauty or fame.
But I believe He did intend for all
of us to know the kindness and
compassion of a friend.

ANITA WIEGAND

Each Day Is Too Short!

I find each day too short for all the thoughts I want to think, all the walks I want to take, all the books I want to read, all the friends I want to see.

JOHN BURROUGHS

Sing for Joy

I will sing for joy in GOD, explode
in praise from deep in my soul!
. . . For as the earth bursts with
spring wildflowers, and as a garden
cascades with blossoms, so the
Master, GOD, brings righteousness
into full bloom.

ISAIAH 61:10–11 MSG

Catch the Wind...

Twenty years from now you will be
more disappointed by the things
you didn't do than by the ones you
did do. So throw off the bowlines.
Sail away from the safe harbor.
Catch the wind in your sails.
Explore. Dream. Discover.

MARK TWAIN

Blessing

Each new day may uncover
something wonderful or something
difficult. The blessing of having
friends is the assurance that we
can rely on them no matter what
the day brings.

A Brighter World

When good friends walk beside us
　on the trails that we must keep,
Our burdens seem less heavy and
　the hills are not so steep.
The weary miles pass swiftly taken
　in a joyous stride,
And all the world seems brighter
　when friends walk by our side.

UNKNOWN

Friends Enrich Our Lives

How in the world does anyone
make it through life without
friends? They're what color is to
flowers. . .warmth is to the sun. . .
and chocolate is to the taste buds.

Give and Take

The relationship between girlfriends is about give and take. At times we give more than we take, and at other times we rely heavily on our friendships—but in a true friendship it all evens out in the end.

ANITA WIEGAND

Garden of Life

The garden of life is always in bloom if you create a place for friendship to grow. It's like giving yourself a bouquet of roses every day of the week.

My Delight

Send forth your light and your
truth, let them guide me; let them
bring me to your holy mountain,
to the place where you dwell.
Then will I go to the altar of God,
my joy and my delight.

PSALM 43:3–4 NIV

Real Friendship

A real friend warms you by her
presence, trusts you with her
secrets, and remembers you in
her prayers.

UNKNOWN

Happiness of Life

The happiness of life is made up
of minute fractions—the little
soon-forgotten charities of a kiss
or smile, a kind look, a heartfelt
compliment, and the countless
infinitesimals of pleasurable and
genial feeling.

SAMUEL COLERIDGE

Be Content

Let me, if I may, be ever welcomed
to my room in winter by a glowing
hearth, in summer by a vase of
flowers; if I may not, let me think
how nice they would be, and bury
myself in my work. I do not think
that the road to contentment lies
in despising what we have not got.
Let us acknowledge all good, all
delight that the world holds, and
be content.

GEORGE MACDONALD

Remember the Laughter

When we reflect on the best times
we've shared with our girlfriends,
we may forget exactly what it was
we laughed so hard about. . .but
we'll always remember the laughter.

Capture Memories

While it's impossible to know the precise moment an acquaintance becomes a friend, there's no doubt it would be a wonderful memory if it could be captured—and there's great probability it would involve two forks and one dessert.

From God

All that is good, all that is true,
all that is beautiful, all that is
beneficent, be it great or small, be
it perfect or fragmentary, natural
as well as supernatural, moral as
well as material, comes from God.

JOHN NEWMAN

Serving

God has given us different gifts
for doing certain things well. . . .
If your gift is serving others,
serve them well. . . . And if you
have a gift for showing kindness to
others, do it gladly.

ROMANS 12:6–8 NLT

Laugh Till You Cry

Every now and then, it's delightful
to laugh with a friend—the kind
of laugh that makes your stomach
jiggle, sends tears down your face,
and causes your eyes to squint so
it's impossible to see!

Roots of Friendship

Friendship is not diminished by
distance or time, by imprisonment
or war, by suffering or silence. It is
in these things that it roots most
deeply. It is from these things that
it flowers.

PAM BROWN

Immeasurable

As we grow, the time between good bouts of fun and laughter grow, too. But its value remains immeasurable—because there are few things in life as important as joy, friends, and the sound of laughter.

Life's Success

To appreciate beauty; to find the
best in others; to give one's self;
to leave the world a little better. . .
to have played and laughed
with enthusiasm, and sung with
exultation; to know even one life
has breathed easier because you
have lived. . . . This is to have
succeeded.

RALPH WALDO EMERSON

Box of Praise

I wish I had a box,
    the biggest I could find;
I'd fill it right up to the brim
    with everything that's kind.
A box without a lock, of course,
    and never any key;
For everything inside that box
    would then be offered free.
Grateful words for joys received
    I'd freely give away.
Oh, let us open wide a box
    of praise for every day.

Real Gift

This is the real gift: We have been
given the breath of life, designed
with a unique one-of-a-kind soul
that exists forever—whether we
live it as a joy or with indifference
doesn't change the fact that we've
been given the gift of being now
and forever. Priceless in value,
we are handcrafted by God,
who has a personal design and
plan for each of us.

Like Him

All of us! Nothing between us
and God, our faces shining with
the brightness of his face.
And so we are transfigured
much like the Messiah, our lives
gradually becoming brighter and
more beautiful as God enters our
lives and we become like him.

2 CORINTHIANS 3:18 MSG

Look for the Best

To laugh often and much; to win
the respect of intelligent people
and the affection of children; to
appreciate beauty; to find the best
in others; to know even one life
has breathed easier because you
have lived—this is success.

UNKNOWN

Loyalty, Truth, and Love

It's not what's on the outside
that makes us worthy, lovely, and
attractive. That kind of beauty is
fleeting. It's that loyalty, truth, and
love on the inside of us, spilling
out unto others, that draws people
to us.

Rekindle the Inner Spirit

In everyone's life, at some time,
our inner fire goes out. It is then
burst into flame by an encounter
with another human being.
We should all be thankful for
those people who rekindle the
inner spirit.

ALBERT SCHWEITZER

Light Within

People are like stained-glass windows: They sparkle and shine when the sun is out, but when the darkness sets in, their true beauty is revealed only if there is a light within.

ELISABETH KÜBLER-ROSS

Rewarding and Beautiful

Some of the most rewarding and
beautiful moments of a friendship
happen in the unforeseen open
spaces between planned activities.
It is important that we allow these
spaces to exist.

CHRISTINE LEEFELDT

Without End

Our lives are filled with simple
joys and blessings without end
And one of the greatest joys in life
is to have a friend.

UNKNOWN

Never Alone

It's impossible to lift something
heavy and laugh at the same time.
That's why God gave us girlfriends.
The joy they bring prevents us
from carrying the weight of our
burdens alone.

WHISPERS OF
Friendship

God's Goodness

God's goodness to us is revealed
in our friendships. They hold
the blessings we were created to
enjoy but can't possibly number—
laughter, encouragement,
compassion, generosity,
forgiveness, and love.

Encouragement

We occasionally have moments
when we're perfectly content
to feel gloomy. . . . Then along
comes a friend who manages to
encourage a smile and can even
send us into a fit of laughter.

Hope and Peace

May the God of hope fill you with all joy and peace as you trust in him, so that you may overflow with hope by the power of the Holy Spirit.

ROMANS 15:13 NIV

Appreciation

The more one does and sees and
feels, the more one is able to do,
and the more genuine may be
one's appreciation of fundamental
things like home and love and
understanding companionship.

AMELIA EARHART

Sense of the Beautiful

A person should hear a little music, read a little poetry, and see a fine picture every day of their life, in order that worldly cares may not obliterate the sense of the beautiful which God has implanted in the human soul.

JOHANN WOLFGANG VON GOETHE

His Love

Meeting a new friend is God's way
of asking us to open our hearts
a little wider, make a little more
time to be thoughtful, and take
a little more time to express His
love.

Something Wonderful

Each of our friends brings
something wonderful into our
lives. It is our gift to them to
encourage their uniqueness, affirm
their strengths, and appreciate the
happiness they add to our days.

Beauty

There is beauty in the forest when
the trees are green and fair.
There is beauty in the meadow
when the wildflowers scent the air.
There is beauty in the sunlight and
the soft blue beams above.
Oh, the world is full of beauty
when the heart is full of love.

UNKNOWN

Girl Stuff

It's important to make time to
do "girl things"—like shopping
trips, afternoon matinees (to
view movies the guys will never
see), and stops at restaurants best
known for their tasty desserts.

God's Wisdom

Real wisdom, God's wisdom,
begins with a holy life and is
characterized by getting along with
others. It is gentle and reasonable,
overflowing with mercy and
blessings. . . . You can develop a
healthy, robust community that
lives right with God and enjoy its
results *only* if you do the hard work
of getting along with each other,
treating each other with dignity
and honor.

JAMES 3:17–18 MSG

Unbreakable Bond

It is a curious thing in human experience, but to live through a period of stress and sorrow with another person creates a bond which nothing seems able to break.

ELEANOR ROOSEVELT

United by Christ

We can share with each other
without being threatened by each
other's differences because we
know that we are united by Christ,
and this union is a union of love.

MADELEINE L'ENGLE

Wrinkles of Friendship

The wrinkles of friendship are
fine creases left by years of sharing
tears and laughter—they are lines
that add beauty and grace to this
wonderful gift from God. . .
reminding us of the journey we
could not have traveled alone.

Shared Experiences

Shopping sprees. Cooking classes.
Chick flicks. Scrapbooking.
Girlfriends embark on joint
ventures because they know how
important it is to infuse their
relationships with laughter and
shared experiences.

WHISPERS OF
Friendship

Certain Things. . .

There are certain things a
girl should always carry when
embarking on a friendship: a sense
of adventure, thoughtfulness,
forgiveness, generosity, laughter,
encouragement. . .and the ability
to make heavenly fudge brownies.

Discovery

I wouldn't trade my girlfriends for anything in the world! They renew my sense of adventure by opening my eyes to the joy of discovering things I would never see for myself.

WHISPERS OF
Friendship

Better Off

You are better off to have a friend
than to be alone, because then you
will get more enjoyment out of
what you earn. If you fall,
your friend can help you up.

ECCLESIASTES 4:9–10 CEV

Anticipation

Anticipating and planning an
adventure with our girlfriends is
almost as much fun as going on
one—even if it doesn't happen,
we have a great time talking about it!

Little Things

Half the joy of life is in the little
things taken on the run. Let us
run if we must—even the sands
do that—but let us keep our
hearts young and our eyes open
that nothing worth our while shall
escape us. And everything is worth
its while if we only grasp it and its
significance.

C. VICTOR CHERBULIEZ

Rejoice

Rejoice in the Lord always.
I will say it again: Rejoice!
Let your gentleness be evident to
all. The Lord is near. Do not be
anxious about anything, but in
everything, by prayer and petition,
with thanksgiving, present your
requests to God. And the peace
of God, which transcends all
understanding, will guard your
hearts and your minds in Christ
Jesus.

PHILIPPIANS 4:4–7 NIV

A Great Friend

A good friend is one who shows
up with chocolate in the middle of
a crisis. A great friend is one who
breaks the chocolate into little
pieces and feeds it to you.

ANDREA GARNEY

Appreciate the Moments

There are endless ways to enjoy
time with our girlfriends—from
the simplicity of a walk to the
luxury of an entire weekend—
and every moment should be
appreciated and relished in full.

Laugh Together

Smiles. Giggles. Out-of-breath,
tears-rolling-down-the-face
laughter. In the company of
girlfriends, it doesn't matter how
silly we look or whether we're
wearing waterproof mascara.
We love to laugh together.

Initiative

[Jesus said:] "Here is a simple,
rule-of-thumb guide for behavior:
Ask yourself what you want people
to do for you, then grab the
initiative and do it for *them*."

MATTHEW 7:12 MSG

An Offering

Take your everyday, ordinary
life—your sleeping, eating, going-
to-work, and walking-around
life—and place it before God as
an offering. Embracing what God
does for you is the best thing you
can do for him.

ROMANS 12:1 MSG

Sources of Happiness

There's no adventure as wonderful as having a group of girlfriends to talk, walk, dine, shop, cry, laugh, travel, or simply enjoy life with— girlfriends are one of the greatest sources of happiness in our world.

Personal Growth

Close friends contribute to
our personal growth. They
also contribute to our personal
pleasure, making the music sound
sweeter, the wine taste richer,
the laughter ring louder because
they are there.

Irish Blessing

May the blessing of light be on you,
light without and light within. . . .
May the blessed sunshine shine
on you and warm your heart till it
glows like a great peat fire, so that
the stranger may come and warm
himself at it, and also a friend.

The Same Direction

True friends don't spend time
gazing into each other's eyes.
They may show great tenderness
toward each other, but they face
in the same direction—toward
common interests, goals—above
all, toward a common Lord.

C. S. LEWIS

Indispensable

So long as we love, we serve;
so long as we are loved by
others, I would say that we are
indispensable; and no man is
useless while he has a friend.

ROBERT LOUIS STEVENSON

Glory of Friendship

The glory of friendship is. . .the spiritual inspiration that comes to one when he discovers that someone else believes in him and is willing to trust him with his friendship.

RALPH WALDO EMERSON

Unique

Don't copy the behavior and
customs of this world, but let God
transform you into a new person
by changing the way you think.

ROMANS 12:2 NLT

As the Angels Give

If instead of a gem, or even a flower, we should cast the gift of a loving thought into the heart of a friend—that would be giving as the angels give.

GEORGE MACDONALD

The Greater Part of Life

But friendship is precious, not only in the shade, but in the sunshine of life; and thanks to a benevolent arrangement of things, the greater part of life is sunshine.

THOMAS JEFFERSON

Whispers of
Friendship

Old Friends

My coat and I live comfortably
together. It has assumed all
my wrinkles, does not hurt me
anywhere, has molded itself on my
deformities, and is complacent to
all my movements, and I only feel
its presence because it keeps me
warm. Old coats and old friends
are the same thing.

VICTOR HUGO

God's Handwriting

Never lose an opportunity
of seeing anything that is
beautiful; for beauty is God's
handwriting—a wayside
sacrament. Welcome it in every
fair face, in every fair sky, in every
fair flower, and thank God for it as
a cup of blessing.

RALPH WALDO EMERSON

At the Close of Each Day

Give me work to do;
Give me health;
Give me joy in simple things.
Give me an eye for beauty, a tongue
  for truth, a heart that loves,
And at the close of each day
  give me a book,
And a friend with whom
  I can be silent.

UNKNOWN

Choose Wisely

Choose your friends wisely.
They will provide the foundation of
spiritual strength that will enable
you to make difficult, extremely
important decisions correctly when
they come in your life.

MALCOLM S. JEPPSEN

WHISPERS OF
Friendship

Fix Your Thoughts

Fix your thoughts on what is true,
and honorable, and right, and
pure, and lovely, and admirable.
Think about things that are
excellent and worthy of praise.

PHILIPPIANS 4:8 NLT

Hugs

Everyone was meant to share
God's all-abiding love and care;
He saw that we would need to
know a way to let these feelings
show. . .so God made hugs.

JILL WOLF

Made Happier

Do not keep the alabaster boxes of
your kindness sealed up until your
friends are gone. Speak approving,
cheering words while their ears can
hear them—and be made happier
by them.

GEORGE WILLIAM CHILDS

Rule of Friendship

The rule of friendship means
there should be mutual sympathy
between them, each supplying
what the other lacks and trying
to benefit the other, always using
friendly and sincere words.

MARCUS TULLIUS CICERO

Friends Make Life Fun

I cannot even imagine where I
would be today were it not for that
handful of friends who have given
me a heart full of joy. Let's face it,
friends make life a lot more fun.

CHARLES R. SWINDOLL

They Understand

Good friends help us maintain a
healthy sense of humor. When we
need to laugh at ourselves, they
make us feel like it's okay. . .and
because they understand, it's never
offensive when they join in.

An Expansion of Oneself

There is one friend in the life
of each of us who seems not a
separate person, however dear and
beloved, but an expansion,
an interpretation, of one's self,
the very meaning of one's soul.

EDITH WHARTON

Search Me, O God

Search me, O God, and know
my heart; test me and know
my anxious thoughts. Point out
anything in me that offends you,
and lead me along the path of
everlasting life.

PSALM 139:23–24 NLT

Best Friend Humor

A stranger stabs you in the front;
a friend stabs you in the back;
a boyfriend stabs you in the heart;
but best friends only poke each
other with straws.

UNKNOWN

Drop by Drop

We cannot tell the precise moment
when friendship is formed. As in
filling a vessel drop by drop, there
is at last a drop which makes it run
over.

JAMES BOSWELL

Just Me

Girlfriend Motto: If you want a
hug, I'll be your pillow. If you need
to be happy, I'll be your smile.
But anytime you need a friend,
I'll just be me.

Friends Make Life Worthwhile

To laugh a bit and joke a bit and
grasp a friendly hand. . . . To tell
one's secrets, hopes, and fears and
share a friendly smile; to have
a friend and be a friend is what
makes life worthwhile.

UNKNOWN

Just for a Moment

There's something wonderful
about making our girlfriends
laugh. Maybe it's the sound we
love to hear—or the joy we feel in
brightening their world for just a
moment.

What Friends Do

A friend doesn't go on a diet because you are fat. A friend never defends a husband who gets his wife an electric skillet for her birthday. A friend will tell you she saw your old boyfriend, and he's a priest.

ERMA BOMBECK

A Better Life

God thinks of us as a perfume
that brings Christ to everyone.
For people who are being saved,
this perfume has a sweet smell and
leads them to a better life.

2 Corinthians 2:15–16 CEV

The Right Kind of Friend

Many a man has been saved from a
life of frivolity and emptiness to a
career of noble service by finding
at a critical hour the right kind of
friend.

G. D. PRENTICE

Room for More

There is always room in your heart
to allow a friendship to grow.
It's amazing how your capacity to
care expands with little effort on
your part. It's like setting the table
for two only to receive unexpected
company. Without thinking
twice, an offer is made to join
you, and the table setting is easily
rearranged.

ANITA WIEGAND

Even to the Least and Smallest Need

Gratitude consists in a watchful, minute attention to the particulars of our state, and to the multitude of God's gifts, taken one by one. It fills us with a consciousness that God loves and cares for us, even to the least event and smallest need of life.

HENRY EDWARD MANNING

Sharing Life

Dear God, thank You for
understanding friends. Thank You
that so often we're on the same
wavelength, laughing together,
crying together, encouraging each
other with our understanding.
I'm grateful that I'm not alone,
that I can share my life with my
friends. Amen.

Hints of the Hereafter

Human love and the delights of
friendship, out of which are built
the memories that endure, are also
to be treasured up as hints of what
shall be hereafter.

BEDE JARRETT

Divine Friendship

The most I can do for my friend
is simply to be his friend. I have
no wealth to bestow on him. If he
knows that I am happy in loving
him, he will want no other reward.
Is not friendship divine in this?

HENRY DAVID THOREAU

Real Satisfaction

Unless each day can be looked
back upon by an individual as one
in which she had had some fun,
some joy, some real satisfaction,
that day is a loss.

ANONYMOUS

Life Is...

Life is what we are alive to. It is
not length but breadth....
Be alive to...goodness, kindness,
purity, love, history, poetry, music,
flowers, stars, God, and eternal
hope.

MALTBIE D. BABCOCK

Let Your Love Grow

Instead of being unhappy, just let
your love grow as God wants it
to grow. Seek goodness in others.
Love more persons more. . .
unselfishly, without thought of
return. The return, never fear,
will take care of itself.

HENRY DRUMMOND

Overflowing Thankfulness

So then, just as you received
Christ Jesus as Lord, continue to
live in him, rooted and built up in
him, strengthened in the faith as
you were taught, and overflowing
with thankfulness.

COLOSSIANS 2:6–7 NIV

A Perfect Day

Memory has painted the perfect
day with colors that never fade;
and we find at the end of a perfect
day the soul of a friend we've
made.

C. J. BONDS

Grateful for Friends

Dear God, I am grateful for the
friends who participate in both
my joys and sorrows. . . .
Thank You for giving us the ability
to communicate our feelings to
each other; thank You for sending
Your Spirit to us through our
friends. Amen.

A Friend Is Dearer

A friend is dearer than the light of heaven, for it would be better for us that the sun were extinguished than that we should be without friends.

JOHN CHRYSOSTOM

Joy and Comfort

I thank God for my girlfriends. . .
for the blessing they are, for the
joy of their laughter, the comfort
of their smiles.

Friends. . .Just When You Need Them

Dear Father, thank You for watching over us, for meeting all our needs. I am forever grateful for the times You place friends in my life just when I need them the most. Amen.

Three Welcomes

May you always find three
   welcomes in life,
In a garden during summer,
At a fireside during winter,
And whatever the day or season,
In the kind eyes of a friend.

Joy in Your Presence

You have made known to me the
path of life; you will fill me with
joy in your presence, with eternal
pleasures at your right hand.

PSALM 16:11 NIV

Solid Friendship

A do not wish to treat friendships
daintily, but with the roughest
courage. When they are real,
they are not glass threads or
frostwork, but the solidest thing
we know.

RALPH WALDO EMERSON

Value to Survival

Friendship is unnecessary, like
philosophy, like art. . . It has no
survival value; rather is one of
those things that gives value to
survival.

C. S. LEWIS

Pick-Me-Ups

We all have days when we need a
little emotional pick-me-up.
Some of the greatest perks come
from the encouraging words we
receive from our friends.

Simple Pleasures

How silent our friendships would
be without conversations about the
simple pleasures of life. They are
the things that become luxuries in
the company of girlfriends.

A Small Smile

They may not need me,
    yet they might,
I'll let my head be just in sight.
A smile so small as mine might be
Precisely their necessity.

EMILY DICKINSON

One Who Loves

One who loves is borne on wings;
he runs, and is filled with joy; he is
free and unrestricted. He gives to
all to receive all, and he has all in
all; for beyond all things he rests
in the one highest thing, from
whom streams all that is good.

THOMAS À KEMPIS

Tapestry of Love

I want you woven into a tapestry
of love, in touch with everything
there is to know of God.
Then you will have minds
confident and at rest, focused on
Christ, God's great mystery. All
the richest treasures of wisdom
and knowledge are embedded in
that mystery and nowhere else.

COLOSSIANS 2:2–3 MSG

Kindred Spirits

The gift of friendship, both
given and received, is joy, love,
and nurturing for the heart.
The realization that you have met
a soul mate, a kindred spirit, is one
of life's sweetest gifts!

Filled with Laughter

Sense of humor;
God's great gift
  causes spirits to uplift;
Helps to make our bodies mend;
  lightens burdens; cheers a friend;
Tickles children; elders grin
  at this warmth that glows within;
Surely in the great hereafter
  heaven must be filled with
  laughter!

Two Requirements

There are two requirements
for our proper enjoyment of
every earthly blessing which
God bestows on us—a thankful
reflection on the goodness of the
Giver and a deep sense of the
unworthiness of the receiver.
The first would make us grateful,
the second humble.

HANNAH MORE

Gladness

May there always be work for
your hands to do. May your purse
always hold a coin or two.
May the sun always shine on your
windowpane. May a rainbow be
certain to follow each rain.
May the hand of a friend always
be near you, and may God fill your
heart with gladness to cheer you.

Those Little Extras

Don't ever let yourself get so
busy that you miss those little
but important extras in life—the
beauty of a day. . .the smile of a
friend. . .the serenity of a quiet
moment alone. For it is often life's
smallest pleasures and gentlest joys
that make the biggest and most
lasting difference.

Through the Common

To live content with small means. . .
To study hard, think quietly,
talk gently, act frankly;
To listen to stars and birds,
to babes and sages, with open hearts;
To bear all cheerfully, do all bravely,
await occasions, hurry never.
In a word, to let the spiritual,
unbidden and unconscious, grow
up through the common.

WILLIAM HENRY CHANNING

The Path of Peace

"Because of the tender mercy of
our God. . .the rising sun will
come to us from heaven to shine
on those living in darkness and in
the shadow of death, to guide our
feet into the path of peace."

LUKE 1:78–79 NIV

Adventures

We live in a wonderful world
that is full of beauty, charm,
and adventure. There is no end to
the adventures that we can have if
only we seek them with our eyes
open.

JAWAHARLAL NEHRU

You've Made a Friend

You know you've made a new
friend when. . . You find yourselves
laughing at the same jokes.
You discover you like the same
books and movies. You find
yourselves talking faster and faster,
trying to figure out everything
about each other. The differences
you find only make the other
person seem more interesting.

ELLYN SANNA

We'll Always Be Friends

Even though we've changed and we're all finding our own place in the world, we all know that when the tears fall or the smile spreads across our face, we'll come to each other, because no matter where this crazy world takes us, nothing will ever change so much to the point where we're not all still friends.

UNKNOWN

An Instrument

Lord, make me an instrument of
Your peace. Where there is hatred,
let me bring love. When there is
offense, forgiveness. Where there
is discord, reconciliation.
Where there is doubt, faith. Where
there is despair, hope. Where there
is sadness, joy. Where there is
darkness, Your light.

ST. FRANCIS OF ASSISI

Walk with a Friend

When good friends walk beside us
on the trails that we must keep,
our burdens seem less heavy and
the hills are not so steep.
The weary miles pass swiftly taken
in a joyous stride, and all the world
seems brighter when friends walk
by our side.

UNKNOWN

"Remember Whens"

Dear Lord, thank You for the special memories I've created with my friends. . .for the little moments in my day when those "remember whens" creep into my thoughts and leave a lasting smile. Amen.

Peace

To be glad of life because it gives
you the chance to love and to play
and to think often of friends, and
every day of Christ. . .these are the
little guideposts on the footpath of
peace.

HENRY VAN DYKE

Surprises

Into all lives, in many simple,
familiar, homey ways, God infuses
this element of joy from surprises
of life, which unexpectedly
brighten our days, and fill our eyes
with light.

HENRY WADSWORTH LONGFELLOW

Always Be Joyful

Always be joyful. Never stop praying. Be thankful in all circumstances, for this is God's will for you who belong to Christ Jesus.

1 THESSALONIANS 5:16–18 NLT

A Breath of Kindness

A friend is one to whom one may
pour out all the contents of one's
heart, chaff and grain together,
knowing that the gentlest of hands
will take and sift it, keep what is
worth keeping and with a breath of
kindness blow the rest away.

ARABIAN PROVERB

Your Heart

The best thing to give to your
enemy is forgiveness; to an
opponent, tolerance; to a friend,
your heart; to your child, a good
example. . .to yourself, respect;
to all. . .charity.

LORD BALFOUR

On the "Replay"

Memories filled with laughter are
the ones we tend to recall over
and over again. They hold the
unique ability to be just as much
fun (sometimes even more!) on the
"replay."

In All Parts of the Earth

Lord, we thank You for the love
   that unites us,
for the peace accorded us this day,
for the hope with which we expect
   the morrow;
for the health, the work, the food,
   and the bright skies that make
   our lives delightful;
for our friends in all parts of the
   earth. Amen.

Love Makes You Stronger

Love makes burdens lighter, because you divide them. It makes joys more intense, because you share them. It makes you stronger so that you can reach out and become involved with life in ways you dared not risk alone.

ARTHUR GORDON

This Little Life of Mine

We don't need soft skies to make
a friendship a joy to us. What a
heavenly thing it is; world without
end, truly. I grow warm thinking of
it, and should glow at the thought
if all the glaciers of the Alps were
heaped over me! Such friends God
has given me in this little life of
mine!

CELIA LAIGHTON THAXTER

God Delights in You

"The LORD your God is with you,
he is mighty to save. He will take
great delight in you, he will quiet
you with his love, he will rejoice
over you with singing."

ZEPHANIAH 3:17 NIV

His Best Work

We may not be featured on any
television makeover shows, but we
can have that same sort of life-
altering makeover on the inside
simply by letting the Master do
His best work.

Lasting Satisfaction

Lord, I may be able to hide the
toll of time for a little while,
but eventually the wrinkles
will prevail. Help me invest my
precious time in more worthy
pursuits, ones that will provide
lasting satisfaction.

Jealousy

Jealousy is such an easy trap to fall
into, Lord. It poisons a household
and distorts reality until imagined
slights become sore wounds.
Please keep me from jealousy.
It serves no useful purpose and
renders me unable to do Your will,
Father.

We Thank Thee

For health and food,
For love and friends,
For everything
Thy goodness sends,
Father in heaven,
We thank Thee.

RALPH WALDO EMERSON

Sticking It Out

Sticking it out—especially when
times are tough—is rare in
today's world. But as Christians,
we should set the example for
beautiful, happy friendships.

Jesus!

Your love will make the God in
you so attractive, people will be
curious about you. They'll want to
know what makes you different—
why you stand out in a crowd.
And you can share the answer—
Jesus!

The Aroma of Christ

But thanks be to God, who always
leads us in triumphal procession
in Christ and through us spreads
everywhere the fragrance of the
knowledge of him. For we are to
God the aroma of Christ among
those who are being saved and
those who are perishing.

2 CORINTHIANS 2:14–15 NIV

A Warm and Tender Hand

When we honestly ask ourselves
which person in our lives means
the most to us, we often find that
it is those who, instead of giving
advice, solutions, or cures, have
chosen rather to share our pain
and touch our wounds with a warm
and tender hand.

HENRI NOUWEN

WHISPERS OF
Friendship

Footprints on Your Soul

Life is full of people who will
make you laugh, cry, smile until
your face hurts, and so happy that
you think you'll burst. But the
ones who leave their footprints on
your soul are the ones who keep
your life going.

NATALIE BERNOT

Let Your Light Shine

The world will be a lot more
beautiful if we let Jesus' light shine
through us everywhere we go. So
shine on, and let the miracle-
working love of Jesus flow out of
you today!

Friends Always

Friends are always friends no matter how far you have to travel back in time. If you have memories together, there is always a piece of your friendship inside your heart.

KELLIE O'CONNOR

You Are Valuable

No matter what you've done or what someone else has done to you—you are valuable to God, and He desires good things for you. He wants to give you beauty for ashes—what a deal!

Read Daily

Read 1 Corinthians 13 every day.
Meditate on the different aspects
of love, such as: "Love is patient.
Love is kind. It does not envy.
It does not boast. It is not proud."
Ask God to develop each of these
attributes in you.

Trust in the Lord

Trust in the LORD with all thine heart; and lean not unto thine own understanding. In all thy ways acknowledge him, and he shall direct thy paths.

PROVERBS 3:5–6 KJV

Blossom

Ask God to give you the patience
and love to blossom—even if
you're among a bunch of ungodly
weeds. Just think, you might be the
only Christian those weeds will
ever see.

Unconditional Love

Make a decision to show
unconditional love to everyone
you encounter. Pretty soon the
world will look a lot better to
you, and you'll look a lot better to
everyone in your world.

A Wish for a Friend

This is my wish for you: Comfort
on difficult days, smiles when
sadness intrudes, rainbows to
follow the clouds, laughter to kiss
your lips, sunsets to warm your
heart, hugs when spirits sag, beauty
for your eyes to see, friendships to
brighten your being, faith so that
you can believe, confidence for
when you doubt, courage to know
yourself, patience to accept the
truth, love to complete your life.

UNKNOWN

Countless Blessings

Dear Lord, thank You for the gift
of friendship. Through this gift You
have given us love. . .comfort. . .
laughter. . .and countless blessings.
Help us to show our friends how
much they mean to us. May we
always look to You for guidance as
we hold these delicate relationships
in our hearts and hands. Amen.

His Favor

Remind yourself on a daily basis
of who you are in Christ Jesus.
You are a child of the Most High
King. You have the mind of Christ.
God has crowned you with His
favor.

The Heart's Hope

Life goes headlong. We chase some
flying scheme, or we are hunted
by some fear or command behind
us. But if suddenly we encounter
a friend, we pause; our heat and
hurry look foolish enough.
A friend is the hope of the heart.

RALPH WALDO EMERSON

Forever Feeling

A friend is a hand that is always
holding yours, no matter how close
or far apart you may be. A friend
is someone who is always there and
will always, always care. A friend is
a feeling of forever in the heart.

COLLIN McCARTY

Across the Miles

Even though friends may be
separated by miles. . .even though
they may go for months without
having a real conversation. . .they
can always pick up right where they
left off. This is true friendship.

Through Thick and Thin

The Lord is there through thick
and thin. . . . Let Him be the
stability in your life. Run to God
when you feel overwhelmed by the
changes going on around you.
If you'll stay grounded in Him,
you'll always be "heavenly hip" and
ready to face anything!

Love Rejoices

Love is patient, love is kind.
It does not envy, it does not boast,
it is not proud. It is not rude, it is
not self-seeking, it is not easily
angered, it keeps no record of
wrongs. Love does not delight in
evil but rejoices with the truth.

1 CORINTHIANS 13:4–6 NIV

May God Shelter You

May the God of love and peace set
your heart at rest and speed you on
your journey. May He meanwhile
shelter you. . .in the security of
trust and in the restful enjoyment
of His riches.

All Things

Remind yourself daily that you can
do all things through Christ who
gives you the strength, and then go
forward and change the world.
You have much to offer!

New Friends

Dear God, thank You for the new
friends You send into my life.
Help me never to think I have all
the friends I need. Remind me
that You have new ways to touch
me through each person I meet.
Amen.

Story of Life

My friends have made the story of
my life. In a thousand ways they
have turned my limitations into
beautiful privileges and enabled
me to walk serene and happy in the
shadow cast by my deprivation.

HELEN KELLER

God's Humor

God often uses humor to show
us He's a real person with a full
range of emotions—and we can
feel closer to Him for having
made us laugh. . . . The Creator
can rain down all kinds of things
from heaven to get His children's
attention and prompt their prayers
and praise.

Love Better

Is life not full of opportunities
for learning love? Every man and
woman every day has a thousand
of them. The world is not a
playground; it is a schoolroom.
Life is not a holiday, but an
education. And the one eternal
lesson for us all is how better we
can love.

HENRY DRUMMOND

Lack in Nothing

Consider it pure joy, my brothers, whenever you face trials of many kinds, because you know that the testing of your faith develops perseverance. Perseverance must finish its work so that you may be mature and complete, not lacking anything.

JAMES 1:2–4 NIV

Think Pleasantly

I have resolved that from this day on, I will do all the business I can honestly, have all the fun I can reasonably, do all the good I can willingly, and save my digestion by thinking pleasantly.

ROBERT LOUIS STEVENSON

I Love You For. . .

I love you not only for what you
are, but for what I am when I am
with you. I love you not only for
what you have made of yourself,
but for what you are making of me.
I love you for the part of me that
you bring out.

ELIZABETH BARRETT BROWNING

Examine Your Heart

It's always a good idea to let
the scriptures be our "spiritual
compact mirror" each day and
make sure we are examining our
own hearts instead of judging
someone else's.

Spend Quiet Time

Spend some quiet time each day
with the Creator of laughter.
Let your heart overflow as He fills
up your endorphin tank, equipping
you to face the serious side of life
with grace and courage.

RACHEL ST. JOHN-GILBERT

Utmost Importance

Love is of utmost importance.
Once you have set your will that
you will learn the way of love, then
there is no flaw or irritation in
another person that you cannot
bear. . . . If this one commandment
were kept—"Love one another"—I
know it would carry us a long way
toward keeping all the rest of our
Lord's commands.

ST. TERESA OF AVILA

Life Gets Better

No matter how bad things may seem, life will get better. God will reset the time machine to FORWARD, and the lovely swan in your future will replace the ugly duckling. And there's a good chance that the best benefit will be your ability to relish the little things in life.

To the End

Love. . .puts up with anything,
trusts God always, always looks
for the best, never looks back, but
keeps going to the end.

1 CORINTHIANS 13:4, 7 MSG

A Friend Who Cares

The friend who can be silent with
us in a moment of despair or
confusion, who can stay with us in
an hour of grief and bereavement,
who can tolerate not knowing, not
curing, nor healing, and face with
us the reality of our powerlessness,
that is a friend who cares.

HENRI NOUWEN

To Have Friends

It is great to have friends when one is young, but indeed it is still more so when you are getting old. When we are young, friends are, like everything else, a matter of course. In the old days, we know what it means to have them.

EDVARD GRIEG

Thank You for Old Friends

Dear God, thank You for my old
friends. I'm thankful for their
faithful friendship. Thank You for
the comfort they give me when the
world seems overwhelming. Thank
You for the laughter they've brought
into my life over the years. Amen.

Share the Abundance

With independence, you get you,
yourself, and, well, you again.
But interdependence gives us
the opportunity to share the
abundance that God has given us
or to receive from someone else's
abundance. And often we make a
new friend along the way.

Close in Spirit

The world is so empty if one
thinks only of the mountains,
rivers, and cities; but to know
someone who thinks and feels
with us, and who, though distant is
close to us in spirit, this makes the
earth for us an inhabited garden.

JOHANN WOLFGANG VON GOETHE

Positives for Negatives

It might be kind of fun to discover a positive for every negative event that life can throw at you. Use the difficulty to your advantage and to God's glory. So go ahead, take whatever is blocking your ability to move forward onto the stage of life with confidence and poise, and use it!

WHISPERS OF
Friendship

Glorious Joy

Though you have not seen him,
you love him; and even though you
do not see him now, you believe
in him and are filled with an
inexpressible and glorious joy,
for you are receiving the goal of
your faith, the salvation of your
souls.

1 PETER 1:8–9 NIV

Love Is Swift

Love is swift, sincere, pious,
pleasant, gentle, strong, patient,
faithful, prudent, long-suffering
. . .and never seeking her own;
for wheresoever a man seeketh his
own, there he falleth from love.

THOMAS À KEMPIS

Little Lamps

My friends are little lamps to me,
Their radiance warms and cheers
  my ways,
And all the pathway dark and lone
Is brightened by their rays.

ELIZABETH WHITTEMORE

Few Things in Life

As we grow, the time between good bouts of fun and laughter grows, too. . . . But their value remains immeasurable. . .because there are few things in life as important as joy, friends, and the sound of laughter.

Differences

God often uses others' differences
to push us out of our comfort
zones. Once freed from our
cozy cocoons, we become open
to experiences that can bless
us, mature us, and give us
opportunities to meet others'
needs.

Friendship and Forgiveness

Dear God, help me to forgive my friends when they seem to let me down. Remind me that only You are perfect; only You can always be there and always understand me. Thank You for all the times my friends forgive me. Amen.

Branch Out!

Do you really think God wants us to live a vanilla-bland life when He's made a thirty-one-flavors world? God wants us to color our world with rainbow colors and Willy Wonka flavors. Sure, playing it safe can make things easier (and duller), but branching out—even a little—can make life fuller (and more fun).

RACHEL ST. JOHN-GILBERT

Greatest Union

By friendship you mean the
greatest love, the greatest
usefulness, the most open
communication, the noblest
sufferings, the severest truth,
the heartiest counsel, and the
greatest union of minds which
brave men and women are capable.

JEREMY TAYLOR

Shared Hearts

Over cups of tea, I listened to my
  friend,
And my friend heard me.
My joy was hers and hers was mine,
As we shared our hearts line by
  line.

ANONYMOUS

Abundant Life

The Creator thinks enough of you
to have sent Someone very special
so that you might have life—
abundantly, joyfully, completely,
and victoriously.

Call On God

Often, life's challenges are like an insomniac baby. We go through all kinds of uncomfortable internal contortions trying to bring peace and rest to situations that wear us thin. . . . The pitfalls of life are unavoidable. Yet, if we become as little children and call out to God, He will gather us in His arms and still our souls.

Surprised by Joy

When we're feeling down, lonely,
or in need of inspiration,
we may find ourselves surprised by
laughter and better able to cope
again. And best of all, we may find
ourselves, as C. S. Lewis wrote,
"surprised by joy"—the joy that
inevitably comes from yielding our
lives to God.

WHISPERS OF
Friendship

Love Is Great

Love is a great thing, an altogether
good gift, the only thing that
makes burdens light and bears all
that is hard with ease. It carries
a weight without feeling it and
makes all that is bitter sweet and
pleasant to the taste.

THOMAS À KEMPIS

Fresh Every Morning

Oh, what joy rises in our souls
as we realize that God's love and
mercy are new every morning!
Each day is a fresh start, a new
chance. Grace washes over us
afresh, like the morning dew.
Great is His faithfulness!

The Gift of Laughter

If we wrestle free to embrace the concept that something about God's gift of laughter is primal and life infusing, we have a fighting chance to rise above the troubles that threaten to steal our joy.

Comprehending God's Love

Dear God, thank You for all
my faithful friends. Their
understanding, their forgiveness,
their love all help me comprehend
your love a little more. Thank You
for showing me Yourself through
them. May they see You in me.
Amen.

Be Transformed

Now the Lord is the Spirit,
and where the Spirit of the
Lord is, there is freedom. And
we, who with unveiled faces all
reflect the Lord's glory, are being
transformed into his likeness with
ever-increasing glory, which comes
from the Lord, who is the Spirit.

2 CORINTHIANS 3:17–18 NIV

Ponder the Possibilities

Today, ponder the new beginnings
in your own life. Hasn't God
re-created you? Renewed you?
Won't He do the same for others?
Feel the joy rise up as you ponder
the possibilities!

Greatest Blessing

The lives that have been the
greatest blessing to you are
the lives of those people who
themselves were unaware of having
been a blessing.

OSWALD CHAMBERS

Kindness Is a Treasure

Guard well within yourself that treasure, kindness. Know how to give without hesitation, how to lose without regret, how to acquire without meanness.

GEORGE SAND

Happiness Comes from Within

Happiness is the greatest paradox
in nature. It can grow in any soil,
live under any conditions. It defies
environment. The reason for this
is it does not come from without
but from within. Whenever you see
a person seeking happiness outside
himself, you can be sure he has
never yet found it.

Forman Lincicome

The Miracle

This is the miracle that happens
every time to those who really
love; the more they give, the more
they possess of that precious
nourishing love from which
flowers and children have their
strength.

RAINER MARIA RILKE

More Than Enough

We can hardly believe it when
God's "more than enough"
provision shines down upon us.
What did we do to deserve it?
Nothing! During such seasons,
we can't forget to thank Him for
the many ways He is moving in our
lives. Our hearts must overflow
with gratitude to a gracious and
almighty God.

Glory of God

Therefore, since we have been
justified through faith, we have
peace with God through our Lord
Jesus Christ, through whom we
have gained access by faith into
this grace in which we now stand.
And we rejoice in the hope of the
glory of God.

ROMANS 5:1–2 NIV

Childhood Imagination

Indeed, now that I come to
think of it, I never really feel
grown-up at all. Perhaps this is
because childhood, catching our
imagination when it is fresh and
tender, never lets go of us.

J. B. PRIESTLEY

Seek Solace

When we're hurting, it's easy
for our mood to escalate from
troubled to traumatized. If
you're going through a tough
time emotionally, physically,
or spiritually, don't wait for your
situation to go from bad to worse.
Seek help and encouragement
early—whether from a friend or a
professional. You may be surprised
at how simple the solution might
be or how much better you feel by
seeking solace.

The Living Expression

Let no one ever come to you
without leaving better and happier.
Be the living expression of God's
kindness: kindness in your face,
kindness in your eyes, kindness in
your smile.

MOTHER TERESA

From the Same Fabric

We are more than just
acquaintances. . .it's as if we are
cut from the same fabric.
Even though we appear to be sewn
in a different pattern, we have
a common thread that won't be
broken—by people or years or
distance.

UNKNOWN

The Spirit of Love

You will find, as you look back
upon your life, that the moments
when you have really lived are the
moments when you have done
things in the spirit of love.

HENRY DRUMMOND

Important Moments

Sooner or later, we all discover that
the important moments in life are
not the advertised ones. . . . The real
milestones are less prepossessing.
They come to the door of a memory
unannounced, stray dogs that amble
in, sniff around a bit, and simply
never leave. Our lives are measured
by these.

SUSAN B. ANTHONY

The Spirit of the Lord

The Spirit of the Lord GOD is
upon me; because the LORD hath
anointed me. . .to comfort all
that mourn. . .to give unto them
beauty for ashes, the oil of joy
for mourning, the garment of
praise for the spirit of heaviness;
that they might be called trees of
righteousness, the planting of the
LORD, that he might be glorified.

ISAIAH 61:1–3 KJV

Comfort of a Friend

Nothing is quite as comforting as
talking with someone who's walked
a mile in your high heels and
completed the journey with her
faith (and sense of humor) intact.

Follow God's Lead

Too many choices at pivotal points
in life can leave us feeling like
confused coffee nerds—mouths
hanging open at the Starbucks
counter. Frozen in time, we may
wonder. *What do I do now? What
if I make a mistake and place the
wrong order? What if I make a fool of
myself?* At those times we need to
take a deep breath, put our hands
in God's, and follow His lead.

RACHEL ST. JOHN-GILBERT

I'll Always Be with You

If ever there is tomorrow when
we're not together. . .there is
something you must always
remember. You are braver than you
believe, stronger than you seem,
and smarter than you think. But
the most important thing is, even if
we're apart. . .I'll always be with you.

WINNIE THE POOH

From Envy to Inspiration

When we see a person we envy or
imagine as living the perfect life, it
may signal that there are latent gifts
within us that we aren't using. . . .
With God's perspective, we can move
from envy to inspiration—from
Stuck-in-Rut Woman to Can-Do
Gal.

RACHEL ST. JOHN-GILBERT

As One

Like branches on a tree, we grow
in different directions yet our
roots remain as one. Each of our
lives will always be a special part of
the other.

UNKNOWN

Trust God to Meet Your Needs

Often when we find ourselves in tough spots, we unconventional ladies get innovative. That may mean making do with what we have until the Lord sees fit to give us what we think will ensure our happiness.

RACHEL ST. JOHN-GILBERT

Wear Love

So, chosen by God for this
new life of love, dress in the
wardrobe God picked out for you:
compassion, kindness, humility,
quiet strength, discipline. Be even-
tempered, content with second
place, quick to forgive an offense.
Forgive as quickly and completely
as the Master forgave you. And
regardless of what else you put
on, wear love. It's your basic, all-
purpose garment.

COLOSSIANS 3:12–14 MSG

Comforting. . .

It is comforting to know that whatever happens in your life, there is someone who will always understand, be there to support you, and help you take on the world.

LORI SHANKLE

Build Your Faith

Don't lose a minute in building
on what you've been given,
complementing your basic faith
with good character, spiritual
understanding, alert discipline,
passionate patience, reverent
wonder, warm friendliness,
and generous love, each dimension
fitting into and developing the
others.

2 Peter 1:5–7 MSG

Create in Me a Clean Heart

Create in me a clean heart,
O God; and renew a right spirit
within me. Cast me not away from
thy presence; and take not thy holy
spirit from me. Restore unto me
the joy of thy salvation;
and uphold me with thy free spirit.

PSALM 51:10–12 KJV

It's the Little Things

The happy glow that
  sharing brings,
A secret smile, a small surprise,
A special look in a
  loved one's eyes.
Comfort given, interest shown,
Quiet moments spent alone—
It's the "little things,"
  small and sweet,
That make loving so complete.

Love Alone

Love alone is capable of uniting
living beings in such a way as to
complete and fulfill them, for it
alone takes them and joins them
by what is deepest in themselves.

PIERRE TEILHARD DE CHARDIN

Deep Hearts

Our Creator would never have
made such lovely days, and have
given us the deep hearts to enjoy
them, above and beyond all
thought, unless we were meant to
be immortal.

NATHANIEL HAWTHORNE

Life Is Short

Life's short and we never have
enough time for the hearts of
those who travel the way with us.
O, be swift to love! Make haste to
be kind.

HENRI-FREDERIC AMIEL

Share All Good Things

If you've been waiting for heaven
to enjoy all the joys and delights
of faith, turn around. Look at the
blessings you've received today,
and all things God has done and is
doing in your life, and appreciate
them. But don't stop there. . . .
Because God never gives us
blessings simply to enjoy—every
good thing is meant to be shared.

Freedom!

There's a special kind of freedom
friends enjoy. Freedom to share
innermost thoughts, to ask a favor,
to show their true feelings.
The freedom to simply be
themselves.

ANONYMOUS

God Blesses the Righteous

But let all who take refuge in you
be glad; let them ever sing for joy.
Spread your protection over them,
that those who love your name
may rejoice in you. For surely,
O Lord, you bless the righteous;
you surround them with your favor
as with a shield.

PSALM 5:11–12 NIV

What Binds Us Together

What binds us together is the
prayer, the promise, and the
lifting of each other's burdens,
the commitment we have made
and kept, to be companions to
each other on the road we share.
What binds us together is the
laying down of our lives for each
other in a way that we cannot even
explain.

ROBERT BENSON

Changing

We are not the same persons
this year as last; nor are those
we love. It is a happy chance if
we, changing, continue to love a
changed person.

W. SOMERSET MAUGHAM

Dissolving Barriers

How it dissolves the barriers
that divide us, and loosens all
constraint. . .this feeling that we
understand and trust each other,
and wish each other heartily well.

HENRY VAN DYKE

Who I Am

Even when I'm stout and seventy,
[my friends will] remember a
little girl in pigtails. They keep
my childhood safe inside their
heads—and when they look at me,
they always know who I am.

ELLYN SANNA

Give It to God

You must hand yourself, with your
temperament,
your frames and feelings,
and all your inward and outward
experiences, over into the care and
keeping of your God and leave it
all there.

The Grace and Love of God

Put together all the tenderest love
you know of, the deepest you have
ever felt and the strongest that has
ever been poured upon you,
and heap upon all the love of all
the loving human hearts in the
world, and then multiply it by
infinity, and you will begin perhaps
to have some faint glimpses of the
love and grace of God!

Inexpressible Joy

So be truly glad! There is
wonderful joy ahead. . . .
You love him even though you
have never seen him. Though you
do not see him now, you trust him;
and you rejoice with a glorious,
inexpressible joy.

1 PETER 1:6–8 NLT

React with Praise

Whenever you react with praise and thanksgiving for an opportunity to grow more like Jesus in your way of reacting to things, instead of grumbling or feeling self-pity, you will find that whole situation will be changed into a great blessing.

HANNAH HURNARD

Carry Them with You

You can kiss your family and
friends good-bye and put miles
between you, but at the same time
you carry them with you in your
heart, your mind, your stomach,
because you do not just live in a
world, but a world lives in you.

FREDERICK BUECHNER

The Lord's Bliss

Lord of hopefulness,
    Lord of all joy,
Whose trust, ever childlike,
    no cares could destroy.
Be there at our waking,
    and give us, we pray,
Your bliss in our hearts, Lord,
    at the break of day.

J. STRUTHER

Be Inspired

Take time in your day to be
inspired by something small—the
scent of a flower, a hug from a
child, an "I'm here for you" from a
friend. . . .Then thank God for the
little things in life.

Surprise Us!

Surprise us with love at daybreak;
then we'll skip and dance all the
day long. . . . And let the loveliness
of our Lord, our God, rest on us,
confirming the work that we do.

PSALM 90:14, 17 MSG

Circle of Influence

The next time you're tempted to covet the good life, think again. Compared to many people, you're probably already living it. Why not try hard to be thankful for all God has given you? Decide to make an impact for Him in the unique circle of influence where He has placed you.

Rest Secure

I have set the LORD always before me. Because he is at my right hand, I will not be shaken. Therefore my heart is glad and my tongue rejoices; my body also will rest secure.

PSALM 16:8–9 NIV

Extend Mercy

The more merciful we are to those
who wrong us, the more merciful
God is to us. And blessings flow
out of relationships that extend
mercy. Want to experience true
joy today? Give. . .and receive. . .
mercy.

Be Content

Be content with who you are,
and don't put on airs. God's strong
hand is on you; he'll promote you
at the right time. Live carefree
before God; he is the most careful
with you.

1 PETER 5:6–7 MSG

I Will Take Care of You

Are you upset little friend? Have
you been lying awake worrying?
Well, don't worry. . .I'm here.
The floodwaters will recede, the
famine will end, the sun will shine
tomorrow, and I will always be here
to take care of you.

CHARLIE BROWN

Be Anxious for Nothing

Be anxious for nothing, but
in everything by prayer and
supplication, with thanksgiving,
let your requests be made known
to God; and the peace of God,
which surpasses all understanding,
will guard your hearts and minds
through Christ Jesus.

PHILIPPIANS 4:6–7 NKJV

Treasures

When God finds a soul that rests
in Him and is not easily moved,
He operates within it in His own
manner. . . . He gives to such a
soul the key to the treasures He
has prepared for it so that it might
enjoy them. And to this same soul
He gives the joy of His presence
which entirely absorbs such a soul.

Share Good News

God has wonderful things in
mind for you. If you ask,
He'll show you what gifts He's
given you and how He wants you
to impact others with them. Don't
wait until eternity to experience
the joys and delights of faith—
share some of that good news
today!

Like a Morning Dream

Like a morning dream,
life becomes more and more bright
the longer we live, and the reason
of everything appears more clear.
What has puzzled us before seems
less mysterious, and the crooked
paths look straighter.

JEAN PAUL

Love Is. . .

Joy is love exalted; peace is love
in repose; long-suffering is love
enduring; gentleness is love in
society; goodness is love in action;
faith is love on the battlefield;
meekness is love in school;
and temperance is love in training.

DWIGHT L. MOODY

Every Day

Try to make at least one person happy every day, and then in ten years you may have made three thousand six hundred and fifty persons happy, or brightened a small town by your contribution to the fund of general enjoyment.

SYDNEY SMITH

United with Christ

If you have any encouragement
from being united with Christ,
if any comfort from his love, if any
fellowship with the Spirit, if any
tenderness and compassion,
then make my joy complete by
being like-minded, having the
same love, being one in spirit and
purpose.

PHILIPPIANS 2:1–2 NIV

Good Character

A good character is the best
tombstone. Those who loved
you, and were helped by you, will
remember you when the forget-
me-nots are withered. Carve
your name on hearts, and not on
marble.

CHARLES SPURGEON

Joy

The God of the universe—the
One who created everything and
holds it all in his hands—created
each of us in His image, to bear
His likeness, His imprint. It is
only when Christ dwells within
our hearts, radiating the pure light
of His love through our humanity,
that we discover who we are and
what we were intended to be. There
is no other joy that reaches as deep
or as wide or as high—there is no
other joy that is more complete.

What We See

We can't begin too soon to try to
understand the needs, virtues,
and failings of those nearest us.
Love should not make us blind to
faults, nor familiarity make us too
ready to blame the shortcomings
we see.

LOUISA MAY ALCOTT

Season of Favor

God takes great pleasure in you
and wants to bless you above all
you could ask or think. So, when
you're in a season of favor, praise
Him. Shout for joy and be glad!
Tell others about the great things
the Lord has done.

Time Management

Effective time management means having time left over to do the things you want to do. It gives you time to spend with family and friends, to be creative and enjoy life.

LEE SILBER

Be Yourself

You simply have to be yourself—at any age—as God made you, available to Him so that He can work in and through you to bring about His Kingdom and His glory.

LUCI SWINDOLL

Living God's Way

But what happens when we live God's way? He brings gifts into our lives, much the same way that fruit appears in an orchard— things like affection for others, exuberance about life, serenity.

GALATIANS 5:22 MSG

Be Joyful

Being playful is a joyful quality. . . .
It reminds you to not take yourself,
or the other members of your
family, too seriously. . . .
It allows you to keep your heart
open to those around you and to
bounce back from setbacks.

RICHARD CARLSON

Watering Others

To make ourselves happy, we must
make others happy. . .in order
to become spiritually vigorous,
we must seek the spiritual good
of others. In watering others,
we ourselves are watered.

CHARLES SPURGEON

Your Success

If the day and night are such
that you greet them with joy,
and life emits a fragrance like
flowers and sweet-scented herbs,
is more elastic, more starry, more
immortal—that is your success.

HENRY DAVID THOREAU

The Me in God's Presence

When I talk with [my friend],
I find I see myself a little clearer—
not the dressed-up me I wear in
public, but the whole me, the me I
take into God's presence.

ELLYN SANNA

Watch God Work!

Cast your anxieties on the Lord.
Give them up! Let them go!
Don't let worries zap your strength
and your joy. Today is a gift from
the Lord. Don't sacrifice it to fears
and frustrations! Let them go. . .
and watch God work!

If I Can. . .

If I can stop one heart from
breaking, I shall not live in vain;
If I can ease one life the aching,
or cool one pain. . .I shall not live
in vain.

EMILY DICKINSON

Making a Melody

Be filled with the Spirit; speaking
to yourselves in psalms and hymns
and spiritual songs, singing and
making melody in your heart to
the Lord; giving thanks always
for all things unto God and the
Father in the name of our Lord
Jesus Christ.

EPHESIANS 5:18–20 KJV

All the Good

Do all the good you can, by all the
means you can, in all the ways you
can, in all the places you can, at all
the times you can, to all the people
you can, as long as ever you can.

JOHN WESLEY

God Is Your Comforter

Want to know the secret of
walking in the fullness of joy?
Draw near to the Lord. Allow His
Spirit to fill you daily. Let Him
whisper sweet nothings in your ear
and woo you with His love.
The Spirit of God is your
Comforter, your Friend. He fills
you to overflowing. Watch the joy
flow!

Live Such a Life

Be such a person, and live such a life, that if everyone were such as you, and every life a life such as yours, this earth would be God's paradise.

PHILLIPS BROOKS

Happiness Is a Sunbeam

Happiness is a sunbeam. . . .
When it strikes a kindred heart,
like the converged lights upon
a mirror, it reflects itself with
redoubled brightness. It is not
perfected until it is shared.

JANE PORTER

Touching Lives

We won't always know whose lives
we touched and made better for
our having cared, because actions
can sometimes have unforeseen
ramifications. What's important is
that you do care and you act.

CHARLOTTE LUNSFORD

Best Harvest

Your best harvest may be the
pleasure you get from working
with family and friends. There's
never a shortage of things to do,
no limit to the lessons that can be
learned.

STEVEN WILLSON

Marvelous Things

O LORD, you are my God; I will
exalt you and praise your name,
for a perfect faithfulness you have
done marvelous things, things
planned long ago.

ISAIAH 25:1 NIV

Love Is Optimistic

Love is optimistic; it looks
at people in the best light.
Love thinks constructively as it
senses the grand possibilities in
other people.

GEORGE SWEETING

From Within

All God's glory and beauty come
from within, and there He delights
to dwell. His visits there are
frequent, His conversation sweet,
His comforts refreshing, His peace
passing all understanding.

THOMAS À KEMPIS

Daily Direction

Lord, direct me daily to accept
and apply the strength that You've
offered, so that I will truly have
the gentle spirit that You intended
me to have. Thank You, Jesus, that
I don't have to do this on my own.

Stand Firm

When you face difficult days,
as all people do, you won't stand
alone. Trouble won't blast your life
but will strengthen you instead.
Your Creator can turn all trials to
blessings, if you just stand firm for
Him. Enjoy your days in Jesus.

Freedom

It is absolutely clear that God
has called you to a free life.
Just make sure that you don't
use this freedom as an excuse to
do whatever you want to do and
destroy your freedom. Rather,
use your freedom to serve one
another in love; that's how
freedom grows.

GALATIANS 5:13 MSG

One Thing...

One thing I'd give my friend, if I could give you one thing, I would wish for you the ability to see yourself as others see you.
Then you would realize what a truly special person you are.

B. A. BILLINGSLY

Reach Out to God

We need to make a conscious
effort each morning to reach out
to God. . .to ask Him to satisfy
us with His mercy, His loving
kindness. If we're truly satisfied,
joy will come. And joy is the best
antiwrinkle cream on the market.

The Art of Timing

Sometimes being a friend means
mastering the art of timing.
There is a time for silence. A time
to let go and allow people to hurl
themselves into their own destiny.
And a time to prepare to pick up
the pieces when it's all over.

GLORIA NAYLOR

Keep the Commandments

Love GOD, your God. Walk in his
ways. Keep his commandments,
regulations, and rules so that
you will live, really live, live
exuberantly, blessed by GOD,
your God.

DEUTERONOMY 30:16 MSG

Walk in Faith

Your heart is beating with God's love; open it to others. He has entrusted you with gifts and talents; use them for His service. He goes before you each step of the way; walk in faith. Take courage. Step out into the unknown with the One who knows all.

When a Friendship Is Formed

We cannot tell the exact moment
a friendship is formed; as in filling
a vessel drop by drop, there is at
last a drop that makes it run over;
so in a series of kindnesses, there
is at last one that makes the heart
run over.

UNKNOWN

Unexpected Joys

Oh, what hope lies in the unseen
tomorrow! What expected joys are
just around the corner. Sure, you
can't see them. . .but they're there!
Before you give in to fear, allow
the Lord to transform your mind.
See tomorrow as He sees it—filled
with unexpected joys.

A Good Haven

To desire and strive to be of some service to the world, to aim at doing something which shall really increase the happiness and welfare and virtue of mankind—this is a choice that is possible for all of us; and surely it is a good haven to sail for.

Lord, You Are My Hope

Lord, You are my hope in an
often-hopeless world. You are
my hope of heaven, my hope
of peace, my hope of change,
purpose, and unconditional love.
Fill the reservoir of my heart to
overflowing with the joy that real
hope brings. Amen.

Cherish

Cherish your visions; cherish your
ideals; cherish the music that
stirs your heart, the beauty that
forms in your mind, the loveliness
that drapes your purest thoughts,
for out of them will grow all
delightful conditions, all heavenly
environment.

JAMES ALLEN

What Matters

What matters is not your outer appearance. . .but your inner disposition. Cultivate inner beauty, the gentle, gracious kind that God delights in.

1 PETER 3:3–4 MSG

Give Joy to Others

To be a joy-bearer and a joy-giver
says everything, for in our life,
if one is joyful, it means that one
is faithfully living for God, and
that nothing else counts; and if
one gives joy to others, one is
doing God's work.

JANET ERSKINE-STUART

Hard Things Become Easy

It is wonderful what miracles God works in wills that are utterly surrendered to Him. He turns hard things into easy and bitter things into sweet. It is not that He puts easy things in the place of the hard, but He actually changes the hard thing into an easy one.

HANNAH WHITALL SMITH

Shine!

Dear Lord, thank You for my
home. I ask that You fill it with
Your Holy Spirit. Even when I
don't have time to polish and
dust, may it still shine with Your
welcome and love, so that whoever
comes in my doors senses that You
are present.

ELLYN SANNA

Daily Duties

Daily duties are daily joys, because they are something which God gives us to offer unto Him, to do our very best, in acknowledgment of His love.

EDWARD BOUVERIE PUSEY

Worth

Feelings of worth can flourish
only in an atmosphere where
individual differences are
appreciated, mistakes are tolerated,
communication is open, and rules
are flexible. . . .

VIRGINIA SATIR

Guard Spare Moments

Guard well your spare moments.
They are like uncut diamonds.
Discard them and their value will
never be known. Improve them
and they will become the brightest
gems in a useful life.

RALPH WALDO EMERSON

Art of Life

The art of life is to live in the
present moment and to make
that moment as perfect as we can
by the realization that we are the
instruments and expression of
God Himself.

EMMET FOX

Sunny Spirit

Humor is the great thing,
the saving thing. The minute it
crops up, all our irritations and
resentments slip away and a sunny
spirit takes their place.

MARK TWAIN

Wait on the Lord

Learn in quietness and stillness
to retire to the Lord, and wait
upon Him; in whom thou shall
find peace and joy, in the midst
of thy trouble from the cruel and
vexatious spirit of the world.
So wait to know thy work and
service to the Lord every day. . .
and thou wilt want neither help,
support, or comfort.

ISAAC PENINGTON

New Courage

The ideas that have lighted my
way and, time after time, have
given me new courage to face life
cheerfully have been kindness,
beauty, and truth.

ALBERT EINSTEIN

Choices

Every morning as we slip out
of bed and slide our feet into
our warm, fluffy slippers,
we have a choice: Will we face
the circumstances and people in
our lives with grumblings and
negativity—or will we face them
with gratitude?

WHISPERS OF
Friendship

Do It Now

I expect to pass through life but
once. If, therefore, there can be
any kindness I can show, or any
good things I can do to any fellow
human being, let me do it now and
not defer it or neglect it, as I shall
not pass this way again.

WILLIAM PENN

Be True

God knew how much the world
needed your smile, your hands,
your voice, your way of thinking,
your insights, your love.
God speaks through you in a way
He can through no other. Be true
to the person He created.

GWYNETH GAVIN

Praise the Lord

Praise ye the LORD. Praise God
in his sanctuary: praise him in the
firmament of his power.
Praise him for his mighty acts:
praise him according to his
excellent greatness. . . . Let every
thing that hath breath praise the
LORD. Praise ye the LORD.

PSALM 150:1–2, 6 KJV

Let Your Gifts Shine!

Our gifts and attainments are
not only to be light and warmth
in our dwellings, but are also to
shine through the windows into
the dark night, to guide and cheer
bewildered travelers on the road.

HENRY WARD BEECHER

Love Looks Like. . .

What does it look like? It has
hands to help others, feet to
hasten to the poor and needy,
eyes to see misery and want, ears to
hear the sighs and sorrows of men.
That is what love looks like.

AUGUSTINE

No One Else

Read, every day, something no one
else is reading. Think, every day,
something no one else is thinking.
Do, every day, something no one
else would be silly enough to do.
It is bad for the mind to be always
part of unanimity.

CHRISTOPHER MORLEY

A Keen Sense of Humor

A keen sense of humor helps
us to overlook the unbecoming,
understand the unconventional,
tolerate the unpleasant, overcome
the unexpected, and outlast the
unbearable.

BILLY GRAHAM

Divine Vitality

Love is the divine vitality that
everywhere produces and restores
life. To each and every one of
us, it gives the power of working
miracles if we will.

LYDIA MARIA CHILD

Sense of Humor

A sense of humor. . .is needed
armor. Joy in one's heart and some
laughter on one's lips is a sign that
the person down deep has a pretty
good grasp of life.

HUGH SIDEY

Simple Charm

The splendor of the rose and the whiteness of the lily do not rob the little violet of its scent nor the daisy of its simple charm. If every tiny flower wanted to be a rose, spring would lose its loveliness.

THÉRÈSE OF LISIEUX

The Best Things

The best things are nearest: breath in
your nostrils, light in your eyes, flowers
at your feet, duties at your hand, the
path of God just before you.

ROBERT LOUIS STEVENSON

Play

The real joy of life is in its play.
Play is anything we do for the joy
and love of doing it, apart from
any profit, compulsion, or sense
of duty. It is the real living of
life with the feeling of freedom
and self-expression. Play is the
business of childhood, and its
continuation in later years is the
prolongation of youth.

WALTER RAUSCHENBUSCH

Lilies of the Field

"And why are you worried about clothing? Observe how the lilies of the field grow; they do not toil nor do they spin, yet I say to you that not even Solomon in all his glory clothed himself like one of these."

MATTHEW 6:28–29 NASB

Peace in the World

If there is righteousness in the
   heart, there will be beauty
   in the character.
If there is beauty in the character,
   if there is harmony in the home,
   there will be order in the nation.
When there is order in the nation,
   there will be peace in the world.

Be My Friend

Don't walk in front of me, I may
not follow; don't walk behind me,
I may not lead; walk beside me,
and just be my friend.

ALBERT CAMUS

Friends Make You Laugh

Among those whom I like, I can
find no common denominator,
but among those whom I love I
can; all of them make me laugh.

W. H. AUDEN

Love Is a Choice

Love is a choice—not simply or
necessarily rational choice, but
rather a willingness to be present
to others without pretense or guile.

CARTER HEYWARD

Every Experience

Every experience God gives us,
every person He puts in our lives,
is the perfect preparation for the
future that only He can see.

CORRIE TEN BOOM

Friends Love Unconditionally

Just thinking about a friend makes
you want to do a happy dance,
because a friend is someone who
loves you in spite of your faults.

CHARLES SCHULTZ

Friends Keep Hearts Strong

Life is a chronicle of friendship.
Friends create the world anew
each day. Without their loving
care, courage would not suffice to
keep hearts strong for life.

HELEN KELLER

God's Plan

It is not part of God's plan that each one of us has beauty or fame. But I believe He did intend for all of us to know the kindness and compassion of a friend.

ANITA WIEGAND

A Smile

It was a sunny smile,
And little it cost in the giving,
But like morning light,
It scattered the night,
And made the day worth living.

ANONYMOUS

Listening

There was a definite process by
which one made people into
friends, and it involved talking
to them and listening to them for
hours at a time.

REBECCA WEST

Preciously Loved

We are so preciously loved by God
that we cannot even comprehend
it. No created being can ever know
how much and how sweetly and
tenderly God loves them.

JULIAN OF NORWICH

Sweetest Support

Thus nature has no love for
solitude, and always leans, as it
were, on some support; and the
sweetest support is found in the
most intimate friendship.

CICERO

Heart Connections

Adventure encompasses not only
the fun times we spend with our
girlfriends. . .but also the times we
make those heart connections over
coffee and dessert.

A Memory

There is nothing higher and
stronger and more wholesome and
useful for life in later years than
some good memory, especially
a memory connected with
childhood, with home.

FYODOR DOSTOEVSKY

Friends Encourage Dreams

Dreams are adventures you invite
only your closest friends to share
. . .for your girlfriends are the ones
who will give you the courage and
wings to reach them.

Count Your Blessings

Count your blessings
  instead of your crosses,
Count your gains
  instead of your losses.
Count your joys
  instead of your woes,
Count your friends
  instead of your foes.
Count your health
  instead of your wealth.

IRISH BLESSING

The Sort of Friend I'd Like to Be

I'd like to be the sort of friend
that you have been to me; I'd like
to be the help that you've been
always glad to be; I'd like to mean
as much to you each minute of the
day, as you have meant, old friend
of mine, to me along the way.

UNKNOWN

Revisit Friendships

Revisiting childhood friendships
could make us better at being
grown-up friends—were we ever
so anxious and willing to help. . .
more excited to see each other
. . .least likely to stay angry or
quicker to forgive?

Diversity

Having a variety of experiences
with our [friends] can help open
our hearts and minds and enable
us to appreciate the diversity God
created.

True Friends

True friends wake up in the middle
of the night for a telephone call,
drop everything if they know
you're having a crisis,
and send cookies through the
mail if they think it will make you
feel better. Their compassion is
priceless—and so is the fact that
we understand how irreplaceable
true friends are.

Everlasting Joy

Therefore the redeemed of the
LORD shall return, and come with
singing unto Zion; and everlasting
joy shall be upon their head;
they shall obtain gladness and joy;
and sorrow and mourning shall
flee away.

ISAIAH 51:11 KJV

Friends Are Blessings

I may find myself looking in the
rearview mirror someday, thinking
about what a wonderful blessing
my friends have been. Or perhaps
I'll be looking ahead, thinking
about the path my friendships
continue to take. Regardless of
the direction I'm looking, I'm so
glad my friends are a part of the
scenery.

Fashioned by God

I have a connection with all my
friends. In different ways they have
helped me grow, made me laugh,
filled my heart with memories.
Each one is a special part of a
single, amazing gift—a gift that's
been carefully fashioned by God.

Merry Christmas

Many merry Christmases, many
happy New Years. Unbroken
friendships, great accumulations
of cheerful recollections and
affections on earth, and heaven
for us all.

CHARLES DICKENS

Christlike Love

Let your love be as wide as His,
With the whole world
  around His knees;
Gather into your warm heart
All His creatures—not a part;
So your love shall be like His.

Good Company

Good company through life's
journey makes the adventures
seem more exciting and the road
easier to travel. I thank the Lord
for my traveling companions!

Joy of Life

Whether sixty or sixteen,
there is in every human being's
heart the love of wonder, the
sweet amazement at the stars and
starlike things, the undaunted
challenge of events, the unfailing
childlike appetite for what-next,
and the joy of the game for living.

SAMUEL ULLMAN

Swedish Carol

We light a thousand candles bright
Around the earth today,
And all the beams will shine
Across the heaven's grand display.

Dear brightest star o'er Bethlehem,
O let your precious light
Shine with hope and peace
In every home tonight.

Comfort in Simple Things

Year by year the complexities of
this spinning world grow more
bewildering, and so each year
we need all the more to seek
peace and comfort in the joyful
simplicities.

Glory to God

At once the angel was joined by a huge angelic choir singing God's praises: Glory to God in the heavenly heights, peace to all men and women on earth who please him.

LUKE 2:13–14 MSG

Endless Wonder

As we grow in our capacities to
see and enjoy the delights that
God has placed in our lives,
life becomes a glorious experience
of discovering His endless
wonders.

Joyful Experience

Have you ever met someone and instantly felt the door open to a friendship? Through a smile or kind word there's an immediate connection. . . . Few experiences in life are so joyful.

Comfort and Understanding

I've faced several situations in my life when the encouragement and empathy of friends carried me through. I never ask God why I'm given a trial; I ask Him to help me remember the comfort and understanding I receive from my friends, so that in return, I can offer it to them in their time of need.

Radiant Joy

Our hearts were made for joy.
Our hearts were made to enjoy the
One who created us. Too deeply
planted to be much affected by the
ups and downs of life, this joy is a
knowing and a being known by our
Creator. He sets our hearts alight
with radiant joy.

At Home

Friendship is where warmth is. . .
where love is. . .where memories
thrive. A place for comfort, good
hugs, and long talks. Friendship
is where grace and understanding
abide. . . . A place where our hearts
always feel at home.

Friends Are. . .

Friends know so much about
giving, yet so little about asking for
anything in return. . . . They find a
great deal of joy in putting others
before themselves,
and none in putting themselves
first. Friends understand
weaknesses, appreciate strengths,
and empathize with hurting
hearts. . . . They are gifts from God.

God Sent His Son

But when the right time came,
God sent his Son, born of woman,
subject to the law. God sent him
to buy freedom for us who were
slaves to the law, so that he could
adopt us as his very own children.

GALATIANS 4:4–5 NLT

Every So Often

A friendship can weather most
things and thrive in thin soil;
but it needs a little mulch of
letters and phone calls and small,
silly presents every so often. . . .

PAM BROWN

Friendship Moments

There's an indescribable feeling
inside our hearts when we realize
we're truly understood by another
person. These are the moments
when our friendships are rooted a
little deeper and made stronger.
It is also a time to thank God—
for He is the one who creates
hearts so beautifully molded
for one another.

Inner Beauty

Why sink into the trap of believing
"beautiful is better"? God is busy
working on inner countenances
that improve with age.
Let's remember that we're in this
for the long haul. Daughters of
the King need never feel inferior
or intimidated, so let's keep this
in mind and be gracious to the
knockouts and plain Janes alike.

God's Unrestrained Goodness

Indulgence. . . Spoiling ourselves.
Unrestrained whims. Who better
to enjoy the luxuries and whimsies
of life with than our friends?
Friendships are part of God's
unrestrained goodness to us,
and the joys they bring to our lives
are one of His sweetest blessings.

Abundant Grace

The Lord's chief desire is to reveal Himself to you and, in order for Him to do that, He gives you abundant grace. The Lord gives you experience of enjoying His presence. He touches you, and His touch is so delightful that, more than ever, you are drawn inwardly to Him.

MADAME JEANNE GUYON

For a Lifetime

The existence of friendship is rather unique; all that is required is a little note or a quick phone call now and then to sustain it for a lifetime.

Pass It On...

God has given each of you a gift from his great variety of spiritual gifts. Use them well to serve one another.

1 Peter 4:10 NLT

Small Acts of Thoughtfulness

There are lots of little ways to
spoil our girlfriends, and these
should be practiced often. From
buying their favorite candy bar
to picking up a book we know
they'll love, we can make their days
special with the smallest acts of
thoughtfulness.

Path to Happiness

When we start to count flowers,
  we cease to count weeds;
When we start to count blessings,
  we cease to count needs;
When we start to count laughter,
  we cease to count tears;
When we start to count memories,
  we cease to count years.

A Garden

To know someone here or there
with whom you feel there is an
understanding in spite of distances
or thoughts unexpressed—that
can make of this earth a garden.

JOHANN WOLFGANG VON GOETHE

Christmas Tonight

Everywhere, everywhere,
Christmas tonight!
Christmas in lands of the fir tree
   and pine,
Christmas in lands of the palm
   tree and vine,
Christmas where snow peaks stand
   solemn and white.
Christmas where cornfields stand
   sunny and bright. . . .

PHILLIPS BROOKS

One Human Soul

A blessed thing it is for any man
or woman to have a friend,
one human soul whom we can
trust utterly, who knows the best
and worst of us, and who loves us
in spite of all our faults.

CHARLES KINGSLEY

Pass It On!

Have you had a kindness shown?
Pass it on; 'twas not given for thee
alone, pass it on; let it travel down
the years, let it wipe another's
tears, till in heaven the deed
appears, pass it on.

HENRY BURTON

God Is All We Need

We're depending on GOD;
he's everything we need. What's
more, our hearts brim with joy
since we've taken for our own his
holy name. Love us, GOD, with
all you've got—that's what we're
depending on.

PSALM 33:20–22 MSG

Joy Will Pour In

The secret to a full and happy life
is to wake up every morning with
the intention of doing as much as
we can to nurture the friendships
God has given us. In no time at all
the joy will begin to pour in. . .and
our days will be filled with His
goodness.

Spheres of Influence

Others are affected by what I say
and do. And these others have also
these spheres of influence. So that
a single act of mine may spread in
widening circles through a nation
of humanity.

WILLIAM ELLERY CHANNING

Scripture Index

Old Testament

New Testament